To

From

First published in 1994 by Michael O'Mara Books Ltd
9 Lion Yard, Tremadoc Road, London SW4 7NQ

A CIP catalogue record for this book is available
from the British Library

ISBN 1-85479-977-0

Cover illustration by Patti Pearce
Inside illustrations by Sally Kindberg
Design by Mick Keates

Printed and bound in Slovenia by Printing House
Mariborski Tisk by arrangement with Korotan Italiana

For a Dear
FRIEND

Michael O'Mara Books Limited

There are ways of saying I love you
There are ways of saying I care
There are ways of saying thank you
For the happy years we've shared.

I say it with a loving look
I say it without end
I say it with this little book
For a very special friend

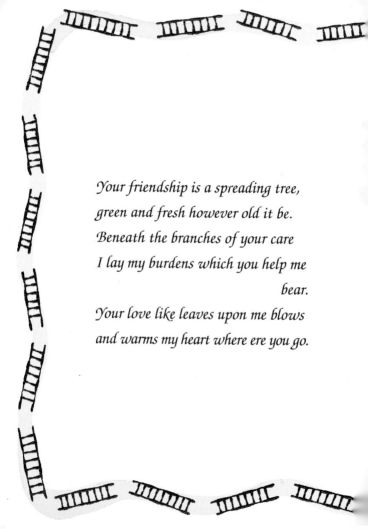

Your friendship is a spreading tree,
green and fresh however old it be.
Beneath the branches of your care
I lay my burdens which you help me
bear.
Your love like leaves upon me blows
and warms my heart where ere you go.

In our busy lives we may forget
To say to those we love the best

Thank you for loving us

In the morning of the day we send
A message to a special friend

Thank you for loving us

And in the evening when we go to bed
We say the words that echo in our
head

Thank you for loving us

You are the friend I like to please,
someone with whom I feel at ease.
You are the friend who with me
                    shares
all my pleasures, all my cares.
You are the friend I like to meet
to talk with, eat with, laugh with,
                    weep with.
And you are the one to whom I send
love and thanks from a special
                    friend.

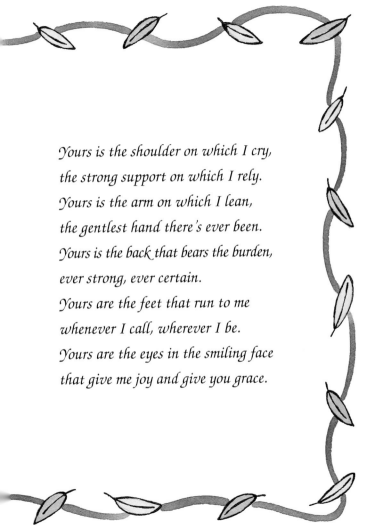

Yours is the shoulder on which I cry,
the strong support on which I rely.
Yours is the arm on which I lean,
the gentlest hand there's ever been.
Yours is the back that bears the burden,
ever strong, ever certain.
Yours are the feet that run to me
whenever I call, wherever I be.
Yours are the eyes in the smiling face
that give me joy and give you grace.

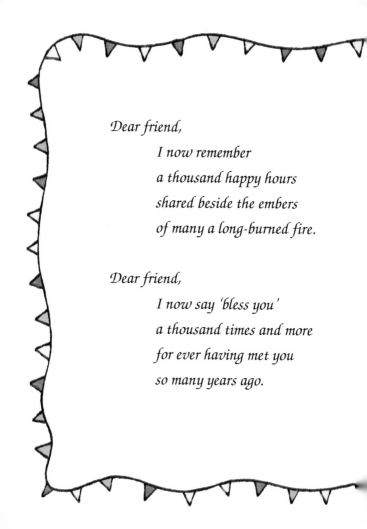

Dear friend,

     I now remember
     a thousand happy hours
     shared beside the embers
     of many a long-burned fire.

Dear friend,

     I now say 'bless you'
     a thousand times and more
     for ever having met you
     so many years ago.

When I had almost surrendered
  you gave me courage to fight.
When I had given up hope
  you gave me the courage to try.
When I lost my way in the world
  you showed me the path I must take.
When I was frightened of failing
  you showed me a way of prevailing.

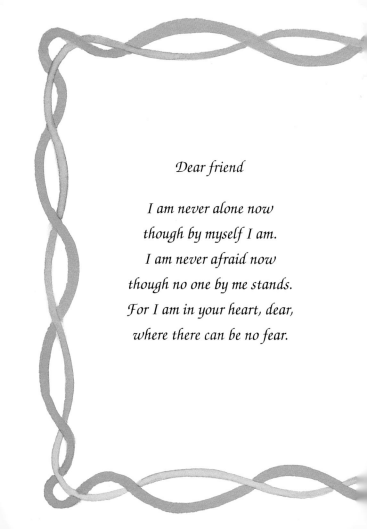

Dear friend

I am never alone now
though by myself I am.
I am never afraid now
though no one by me stands.
For I am in your heart, dear,
where there can be no fear.

Dearest friend
What shall I do in times of strife?
Turn to you

Dearest friend
How can I give meaning to my life?
Turn to you

Dearest friend
What shall make my joy complete?
Turn to you

Dearest friend
How shall I my promise keep?
Turn to you

Friendship
>   is the key in the door
>   that leads to the garden of love.

Friendship
>   is the star at evening,
>   the first light in the night sky.

Friendship
>   is the candle burning bright,
>   the flame that never falters.

Friendship
>   is the leap of my heart
>   when I hear your knock on the door.

You are my special friend
for every season of the year:

When cherry trees their blossom bear
and in the summer when the roses
                    bloom,
but most I need you when the
                    autumn rain
beats fiercely on the windowpane.
And when at last old winter scowls
and blows down gales upon your
                    boughs,
still, dearest friend, you do not bend.

You are my special friend indeed,
you never promise what you cannot do
nor ever deny me the time I need
though so many others want you too.

All I can promise, dearest friend,
is my true love which in this book I
send.